SCRIBUS
Quick And Easy Learning

SCRIBUS

Quick And Easy Learning

By

Lunarion Graphic

2023

Contents

INTRODUCTION

In Graphic Design, layout is a fundamental thing to learn.

Scribus is a Book Layout Design Application, A Free alternative to the Adobe InDesign application.

There is no doubt that applications suitable for book layout are dominated by Adobe InDesign; We all know that this is a very extensive and advanced software. However, Scribus has one advantage, namely that it is free.

You can download it on the official site on the Internet, as well as on various community sites.

Lunarion

Book layout with Scribus

However, for some time now, free alternatives have emerged that, while not altering InDesign, are more than adequate for doing rather complex layout work. The free book and magazine publishing Softwares that we know of are: Scribus, Joomag, PagePlus and LucidPress, although of course there are several more. In other previously published posts we have provided a short review of LucidPress highlighting its great usability, but this time we want to introduce you to Scribus: we have taken a look at this veteran software and it can really be an alternative to drafting books in InDesign , so there are fewer in books that don't require very complex layouts.

Download Scribus.

Downloading Scribus in full and portable version can be done without any difficulty from this link: *https://www.scribus.net/downloads/*

Installing Scribus

After installing the appropriate version for our operating system (in our case Windows 7 64 bit), we open the program and see that the new document window allows us to show margins and also indentation (well, it is already more than a word that allows as a program) . layout). We will indicate an indentation of 3 mm (which we usually recommend to our clients).

1.STARTING SCRIBUS

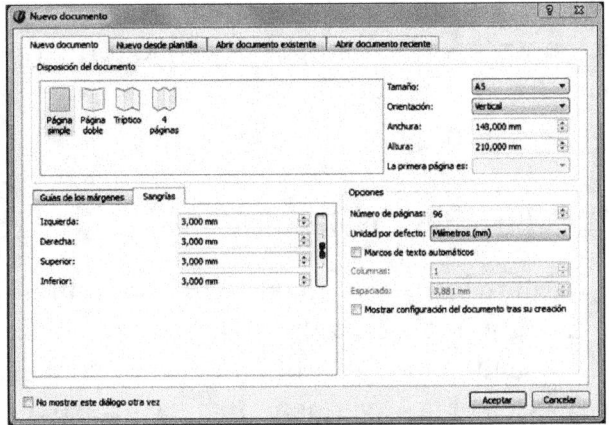

By default, the program offers 4 layout options: single page, double page, triptych and "4 pages", as well as options for indicating the number of pages in the document and the size and orientation of regular pages.

How offset printing works: a detailed guideIf we wanted to lay out a 96-page book in A5 format, for example, we would indicate:

At this point it is also important to check the "automatic text frame" option, because this way we will not have to create a new text frame every time we want to write.

We click "OK" and we already have our document, ready to import text and format it.

Book layout in Scribus

By following the typical steps in putting together a book: creating styles and master pages and applying both to the document, we will get a document that is effectively formatted and ready to export as a PDF to take to the Print Shop.

The practice publications in this tutorial are designed for US letter size paper or international A-4 paper. Instructions apply to both document sizes.

1.Write text

First draw box , Click

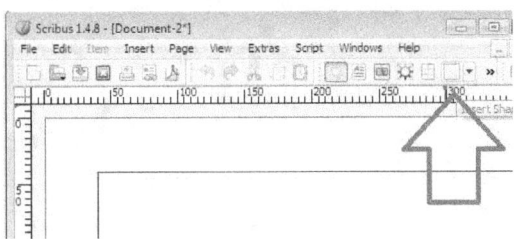

First draw the Box area. Click the Square box tool from the Tool box.

Then Click+Hold on the screen and move the mouse to the desired box size and click again.Convert the box into a text field by:

Menu: *Item>Convert to>Text Frame*

Then we can write in the box or by Edit Text (Ctrl+T)

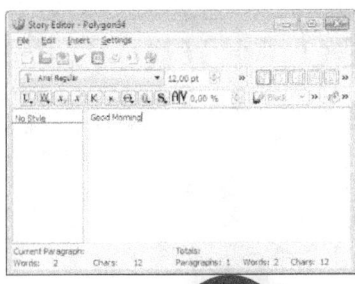

2. Create a shape with the pen tool

To create a curve shape, click the "Pen Tool" with the following pen eye image:

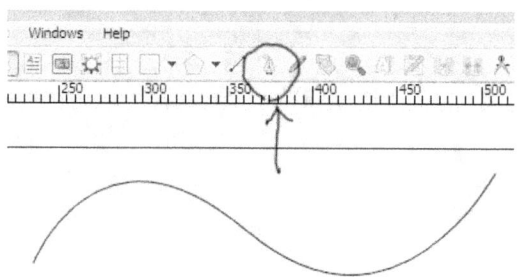

3, Putting Text On The Curve

Create simple text and a curve, then select both.

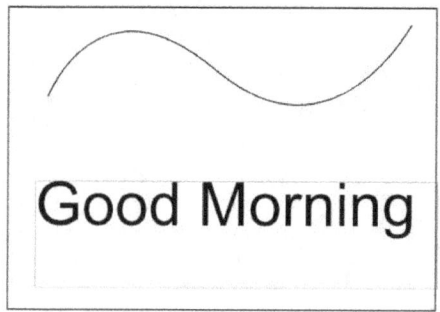

Then select the Item menu then Attach to Path

Menu: *Item>Attach to Path*

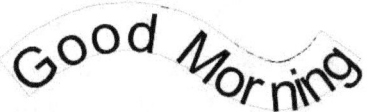

4. Attaching Text Into Shape

Create with PenTool to form a simple shape, then select the shape.

Menu: *Item>Convert to>Polygon*

Then Menu: *Item>Convert to>Text Frame*

Click on the shape then look for the .txt file as the required script, by selecting Menu: *File > Import > Get text* or *(Ctrl + D)*

or right click Get text.

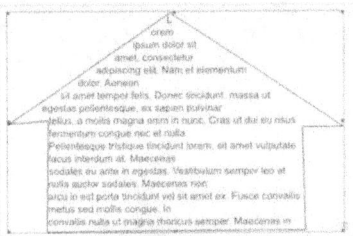

5. Attach the image into the shape

Select thye Shape,

Menu: *Item>Convert to>Polygon*

Menu: *Item>Convert to>Image Frame*

Click on the shape then look for the required .svg, .eps, .ai, .pdf, .jpg or .png image file,

by selecting Menu: *File > Import > Get Image (Ctrl + D)*

or right click *Get Image.*

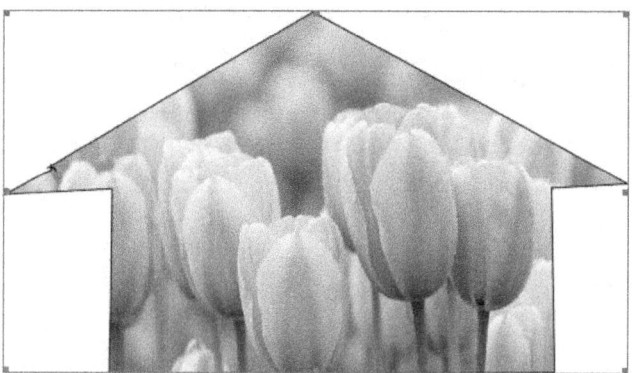

6. Insert a shape between the text

How to insert a shape between text is as follows.

Select the Shape above the text and select the "USE FRAME SHAPE" menu from the Property Box.

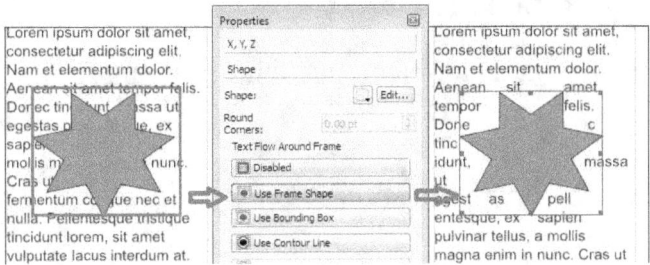

Menu: *Windows>Properties>Shape>Use FrameShape*

7. Flowing the Manuscriptto Another Frame

If your article consists of several columns, then you need several text frames. So that the text frame continues the contents of the first text frame article, click the first text frame, click the following tool and click the next text frame.

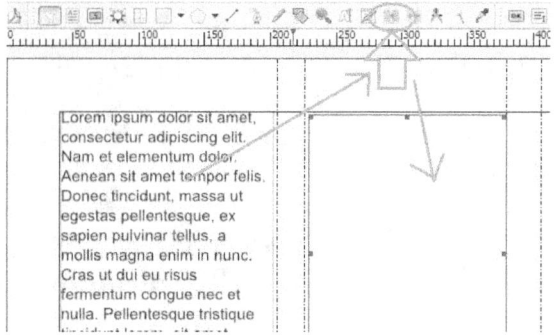

8, Rotate the Object

To rotate an object, use the following tool.

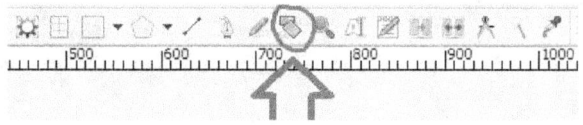

Objects that can be rotated are text, images, shapes or any object. An example in this case is text.

Or for more precise rotation use:

Tool Property > Rotate.

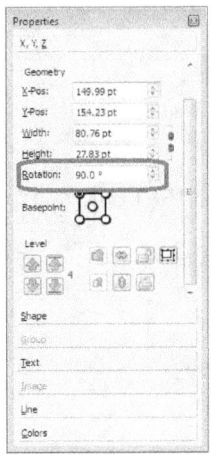

9. Adding New Colors To The Palette

Menu: *Edit>Color>*

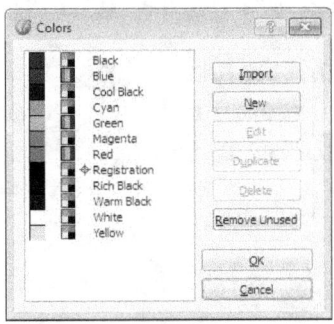

Then in the Color dialog box select *New*

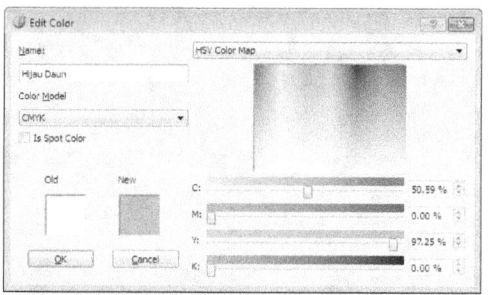

Make the color as you like, in this case I made it green,

Create Color Shapes

Create the default shape of a box or other shape with PenTool to form a simple shape, then select the shape.

Menu: Item>*Convert to>Polygon*

Color it with the color from the property (F2) Leaf Green, with the color in the Property color menu palette.

\

Menu: Property > Color

o

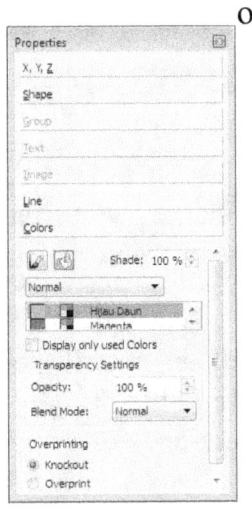

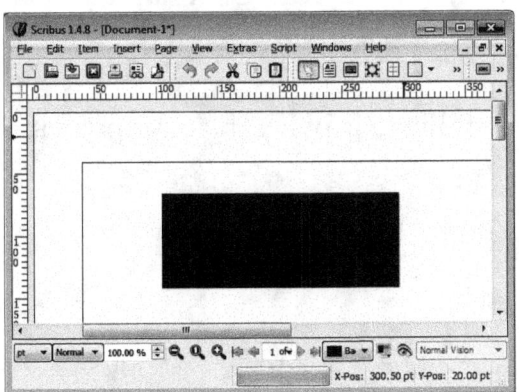

2. CREATE A LETTERHEAD

When you start a new publication, you first create the publication's page characteristics (size, orientation,

tion, and margins), whether it will be printed on one side or two, and the printer you will use for the final version

content of your publication.

Double-click the SCRIBUS Trial icon.

You will see SCRIBUS startup

screen, followed by a blank application window.

Menu: File > New.

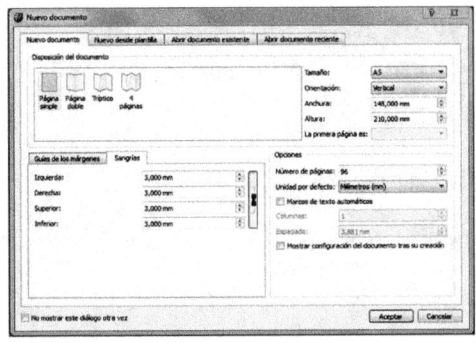

Select the Single Page Option.

Click in the margin text box and set these margins:

Left: 40 pt

Right: 40 pt

Top: 40 pt

Bottom: 40 pt

The best way to learn SCRIBUS is to try it yourself. This tutorial walks you through some basic SCRIBUS skills as you create and

printing letterheads and brochures for comics, for example the fictional company "HAPPY SHOP (Hs)".

You will learn how to:

Type and format text, and define text styles.

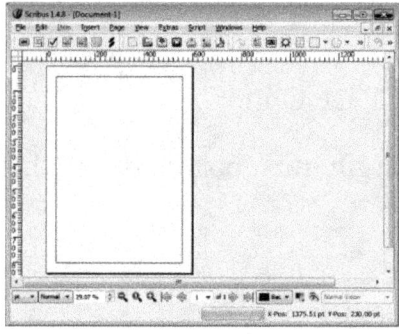

1. Ruler Guide

SCRIBUS provides a non-print guide to help you

Align and position objects on the page. Pages already have margin guides—dotted or colored rectangles that represent the page margins that you specify in the Document Setup dialog box. Now you will

Added Ruler Guides To add ruler guides:

Make sure there is a check mark next to Show The Rulers, Show Guides, and Snap to Rulers commands are active submenu Guides and Rulers pada menu :

Menu:

View >Show Ruler. (Ctrl + Shift + R)

When Snap to Rulers is selected, SCRIBUS will draw hover over the row with each tick

mark on the ruler whenYou create your guide. This ensures proper placement of the

ruler guide.

Press *Ctrl + 1 (Real Size)*

This action centers your view in the top left cornerpage and change the page view to 100% actual size page, so you can place the ruler guides precisely.

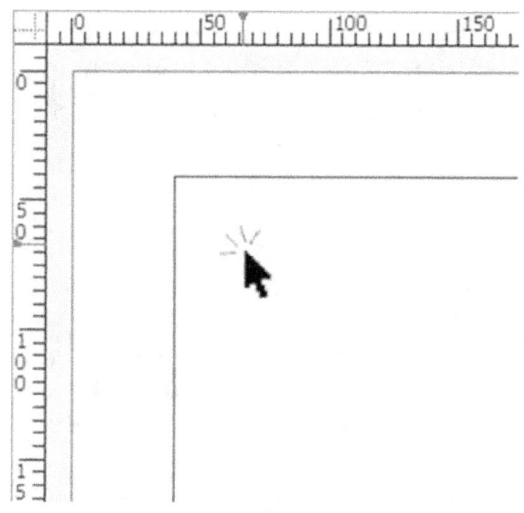

Enlarged view in the top left corner of the page. Position the pointer on the horizontal ruler (which extends across the top of the publication window) and drag it down to 1

-inch (3.2 cm) markings on the vertical

ruler. The horizontal ruler guide appears.

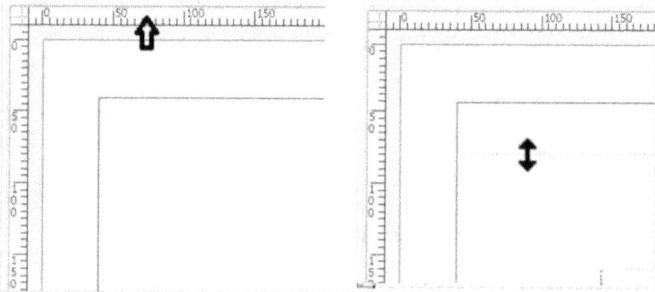

As you click and drag…the pointer changes to a from here…two-way arrow until you release the mouse button.

Use the scroll bar or hand grip to move the view to the bottom left corner of the page. to use the grasping hand, hold down the Alt (Windows) key while you press the mouse button, then drag the grasping hand. Create three more ruler guides as follows:

Drag the vertical guide to inch mark on

horizontal ruler. Drag the vertical guide to

inch mark on

horizontal ruler.

Drag the horizontal guide to 9

inch mark on

vertical ruler.

Drag the first vertical guide

Drag the second vertical guide

Drag the horizontal guide

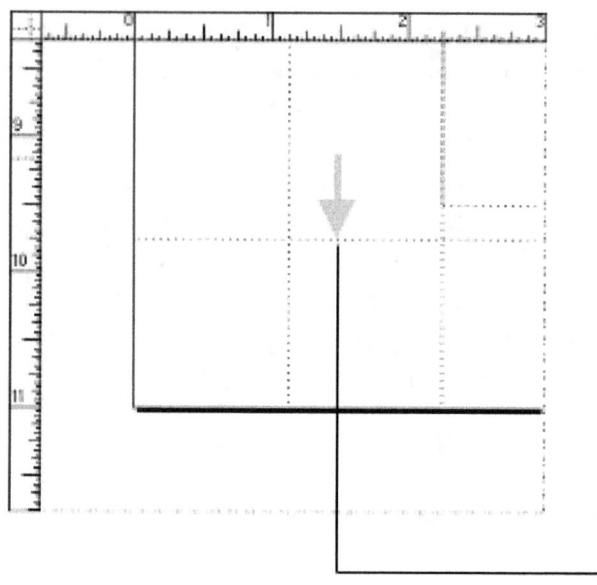

Lock Guides

Select Check Lock Guides from Guides and Rulers in the lower left corner.

Menu: *Page > Manage Guide > Guide Manager.*

.

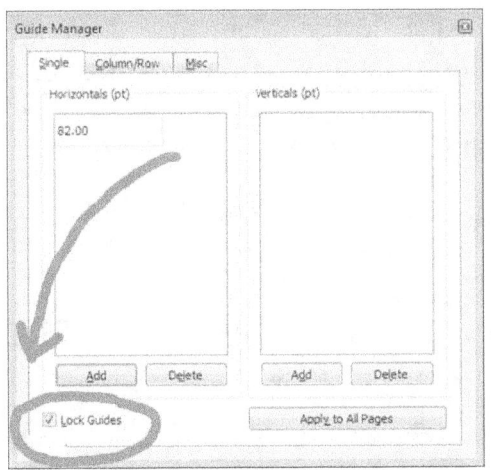

When Lock Guides is selected, SCRIBUS
locks the guide ruler in place, so you cannot
accidentally change its position.

2. Typing Text

for the letterhead you create here, you will
type an advertisement for a fictitious shop
called Happy Shop"Hs".

First, you'll set text defaults—formatting
that SCRIBUS applies to each new block of
text you create.

If the master page icon (in the lower left
corner of the publication window) is black,
you are working on a master page, which

contains basic design elements, such as page numbers, that are common to most or all pages in your publication. Click the page 1 icon to go to page 1.

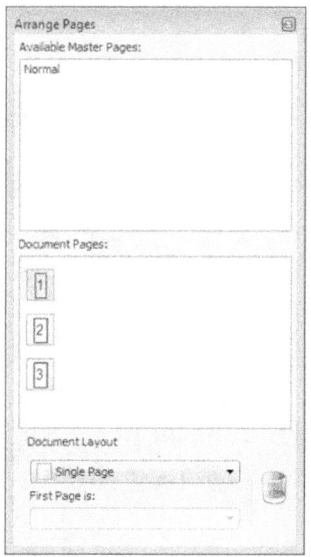

To type text:

The Helvetica font is used in this illustrative example from MAC. If you work on Windows, you can replace Arial, which is similar to Helvetica.

Select Size 200% from the Look in submenu

Menu: View > Size 200%.

Use the scroll bar or hand grip to move to bottom left corner of the page.

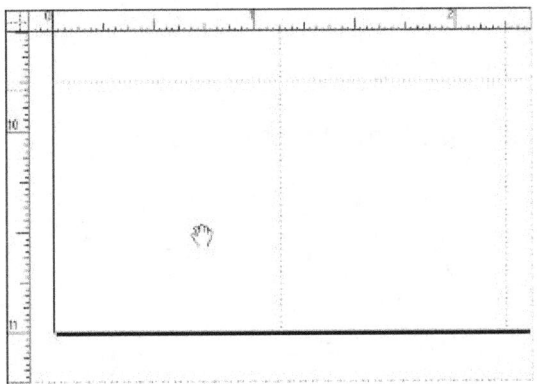

Select the text tool from the toolbox.

The pointing device changed to an I-beam. You are now ready to create a text block for the text you will type.

Position the small horizontal check mark on the I-beam at the intersection of the leftmost vertical guide and the horizontal guide at the bottom of the page.

Drag the I-beam down and to the right until you intersect the next vertical ruler guide, as shown below, and then release the mouse button.

This creates a block of text that controls the width of the text file.

Drag it from here…

The flashing cursor indicates

insertion point for the text you type

here

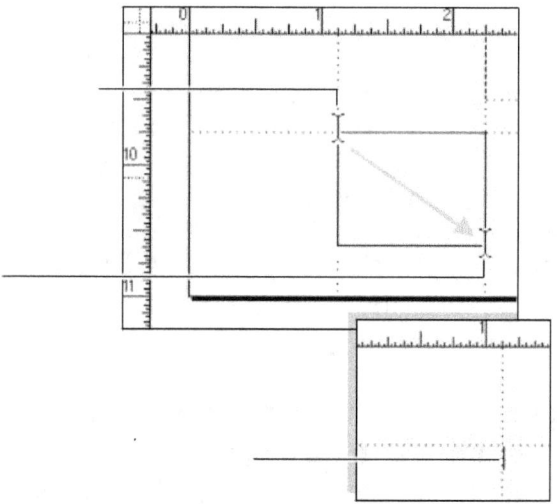

Type the street address shown below, then press ENTER, after each line to create a new line.

If the text wraps to the next line, select the pointer tool, click on the block of text, then drag the right corner handle to the right until the text fits on the line.

If your text block is not positioned as shown, select the pointing tool, and click inside the text block to select it. Drag the block as necessary to align the text within its margins as shown.

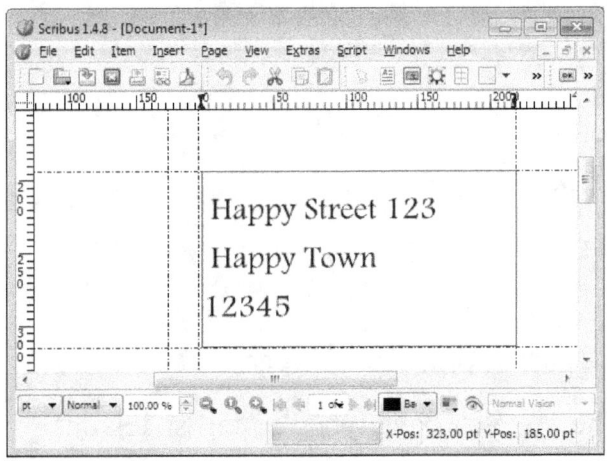

If a down arrow appears in the bottom window shade of the handle, drag it down to reveal all the text in the block.

When the handle is empty, there is no additional text for it reveal.

Top edge

in line with the horizontal guide

Right edge

in line with the vertical guide

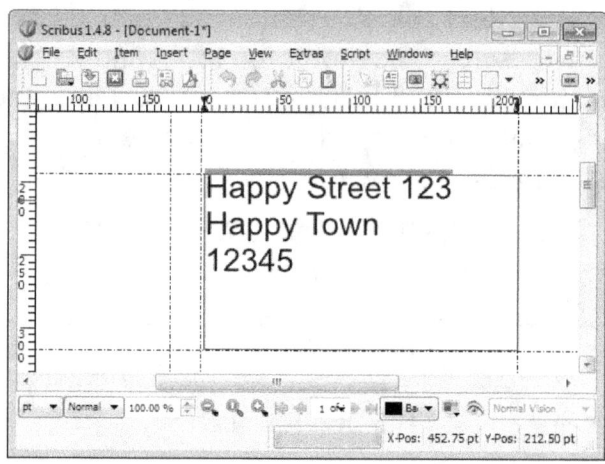

3. Formatting Text Characters

The text you have typed so far is Helvetica 7 points

10-point leading (vertical distance between two lines of text). That's because you previously selected 7 point Helvetica as the default size and font and 10 point as the default reference.

You can select any text in a publication and use commands in the Type menu to apply formatting different from the default. In this exercise, you will practice text formatting.

To Format Text:

menu : Edit> *Styles* > *Style Manager.*

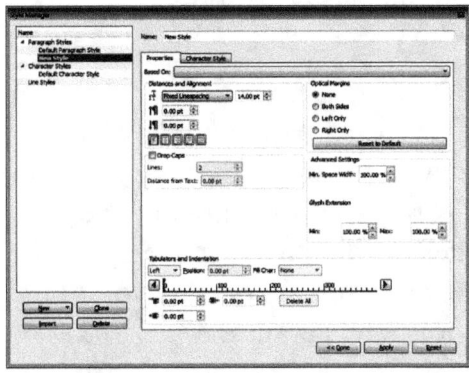

Text with 10 leading pointsText with 14 leading points

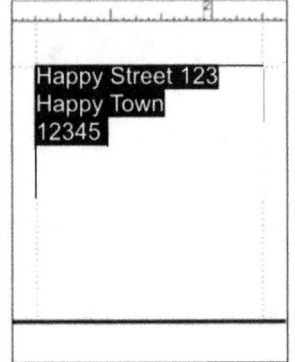

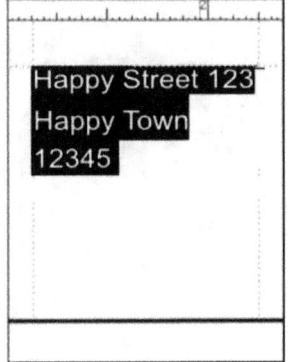

5. Formatting Paragraphs

Certain formatting decisions, such as alignment (centered or justified, for example), indentation, and tab position, apply to the entire paragraph. to format graphics, you must use text tools.

You can format a paragraph by triple-clicking anywhere in the paragraph to select the paragraph or clicking Service point anywhere in the paragraph. SCRIBUS starts a new paragraph every time you press ENTER. to format a paragraph:

If an address is not already selected, select some

of all three paragraphs in the address by dragging the text tool from the first line to the last line.

Select Align Center

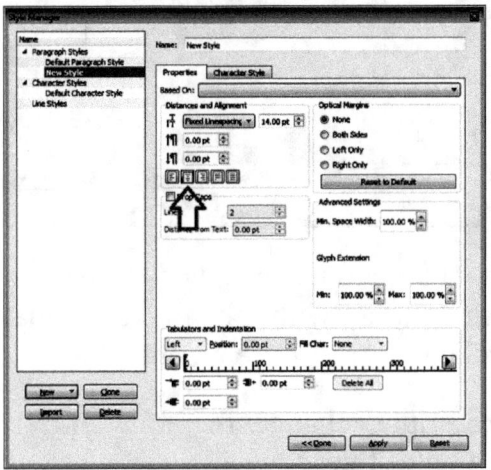

Align Left align Centre

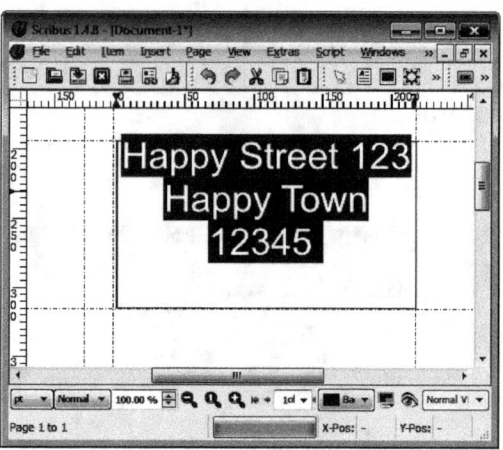

If you like, you can spend a few minutes experimenting with the text formatting commands on the Type menu.

For example, change the font and size, or try out type styles.

6. Draw a Box

Now you will draw a black box around the address to add visual appeal. to draw a box:

Select the rectangle tool from the Tool box.

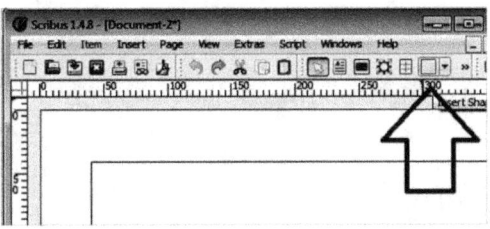

When you move the pointer across the page, it becomes a crossbar.

Select 1 pt from the Lines submenu in Elements

Menu : *Windows > Property > Line > 1 pt.*

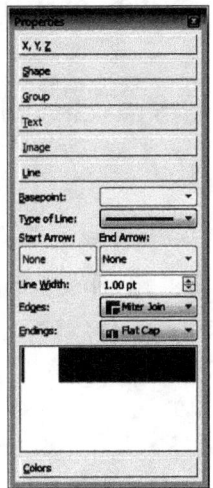

This sets the line thickness (or weight) for the box

You will draw.

By selecting a formatting option from the Elements menu before you start drawing, and without seeing anything selected, you set the default formatting for all new objects

you add to a publication or template.

Use the default format by selecting an object and changing its formatting, or you can set a new default by

selects formatting options without selected objects.

to draw a box, click on the crossbar

intersection of the ruler guides at the top left corner of the text block, then drag it to the bottom right of the text block, as shown below. Drag it from here…to here.

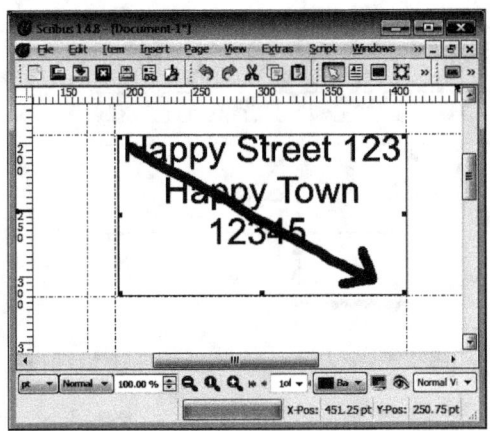

\

If you align the box exactly with a ruler
guide, it may be difficult to distinguish the
top and sides

box from the ruler guide.

Select Show Guides from the Guides and
Rulers submenu

menu :View> *Ruler* >*Show Rule*r) to hide
or displays the ruler guide.

7. Drawing Lines

Now you will draw two horizontal lines in
the box you created used to separate
address lines. to draw a line:

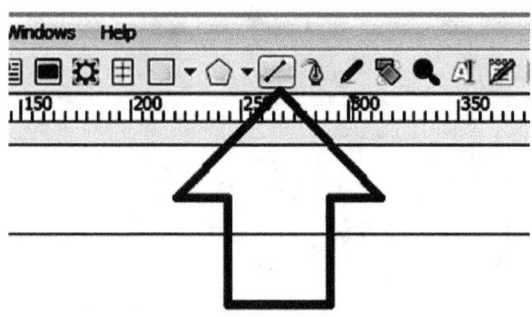

Select the limited line tool in the toolbox.

Click the bar on the left side of the box below the first line of the address, then drag it to the right side of the box, as shown below. Repeat to draw a line below the second line of addresses.

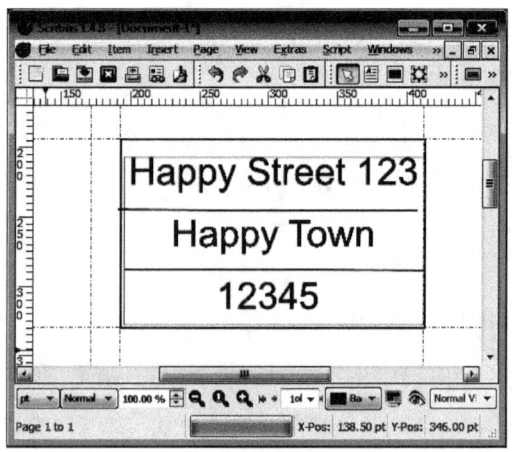

Drag it from here…

Repeat for the second row below the city and state here

8. Importing Pictures

SCRIBUS offers various ways to manage graphics in your publications. In this exercise, you will place a graphic from another application into your publication to use as a company logo.

In this exercise, you will place your company logo at the top of your letterhead.

Select Actual Size from the View in submenu

Menu: *View > 100%* (or *Ctrl+1*).

to place a logo graphic:

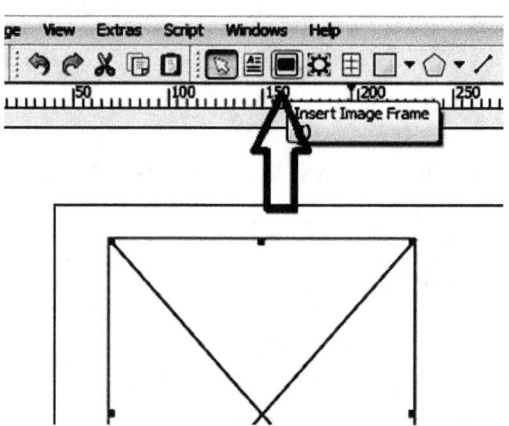

Gunakan Tool Insert Image frame pada toolbox.

Pilih Menu: File > Import> Get Image (Ctrl + D)

or right click Get Image file Logo.tif , then click OK

Click near the top of the page to place the logo.

While the logo is still selected, position the pointer tool in the center of the logo, click, and drag it into alignment with the top and leftmost ruler guides.

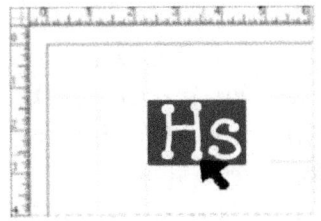 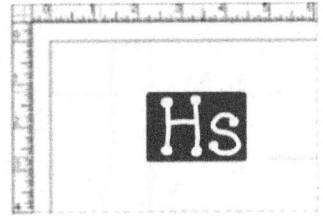

When you move an object, the cursor changes to a four-way arrow.

9. Resizing Images

In this exercise, you will resize the graphic you just placed,

maintains its original proportions to fit neatly between the two vertical ruler guides you created earlier. to change the chart size:

Using the pointing tool, select the graphic if not all are ready to be selected.

Hold down the Shift key, click the bottom right handle of the graph, and drag it to the rightmost vertical of the ruler guide.

Notes:

Pressing the Shift key as you drag ensures that SCRIBUS maintains the graphic's original proportions as you resize it. You have to release the mouse button before you release the Shift key for this to work.

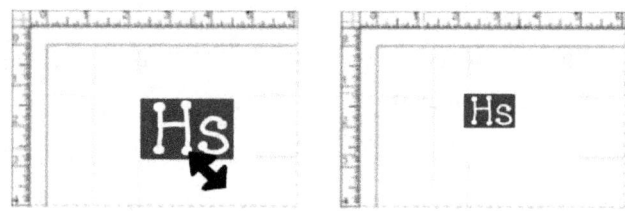

While holding down the Shift key,… then align between the graph size… two vertical rulers.

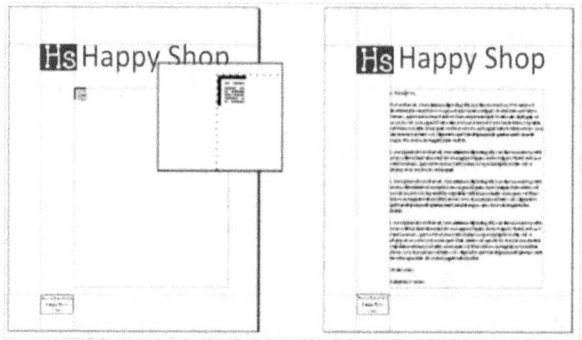

Congratulations on completing your first SCRIBUS publication! You have combined text and graphics for created a simple letterhead for the Happy Shop, a fictional garden center. Now we'll show you how to easily use the publications you create

9, Placing the Letter on Letterhead

Leave your publication open while you prepare to place the text file on the letterhead page. Placing text is similar to placing graphics. to place a text file:

Select Fit in Window

Menu:*View > Fit height.*

Select the Insert Text Frame Icon from the toolbox.

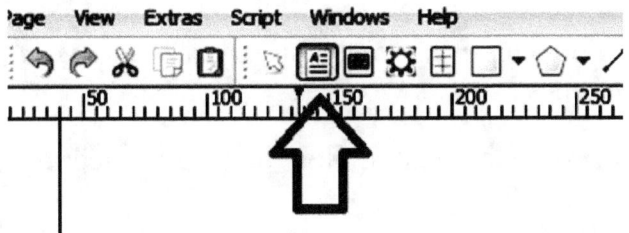

Pilih Import dari Menu: File > Import> Get Text (Ctrl + D)

or right click Get Text.

Look for the required Manuscript Text.

Position the loaded text icon as shown in the following illustration. Once the text flows onto the letterhead, it has a window handle indicating that it is selected. If the down arrow is on the bottom window handle, drag it down

reveals all the text in the block. When the handle is empty, the text block contains no additional text.

When you click loaded... the story flows into the text icon here... page.

You are now ready to print the letterhead you created.

 You can print one copy each time you open

Print Document dialog box (by selecting *File > Print*).

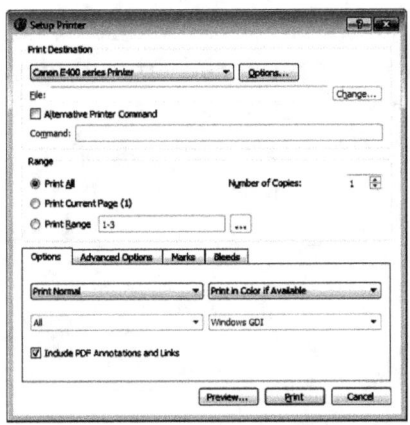

Select the active printer name for the Printer option.

This printer can be one that you specify in the Document Setup dialog box for the final print of your publication, or it can be a desktop printer as a proof copy.

Click *Print.*

You have successfully printed your letterhead. Publication is open so you don't lose your work. Although

Now that you have successfully completed the letterhead,

You are ready to create a brochure. The next section of this tutorial introduces several design techniques, such as manipulating type and arranging graphics and text, that show how you can use SCRIBUS to convey powerful messages on the page.

3. CREATE A FLYER

Now that you've learned some SCRIBUS fundamentals, we'll walk you through additional technical technologies that are important for creating distinctive publicity. You'll create a flyer for a fictional client, Happy Shop, as you learn how to:

Work with master pages to provide a consistent look

 for a publication.

-

Create, import, rotate, and resize objects.

-

Overlapping text and graphics.

-

Work with text in the story editor.

-

Work with several open publications.

-

Print publications.

CRIBUS comes with several prebuilt templates

including page design, text styles, and text and graphics

placeholders to simplify your work.

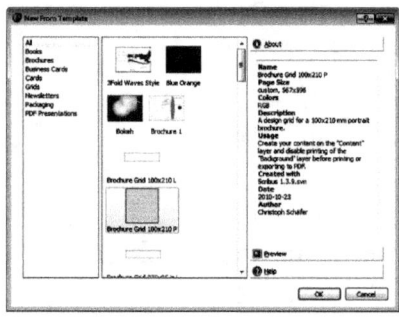

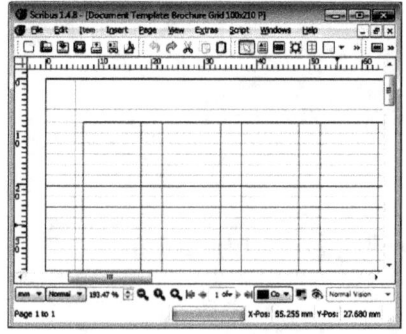

Template for brochure

SCRIBUS templates offer two main benefits: they

provides a fast and easy way to create professionally designed designs

document, and you can use it over and over again to create

lish a consistent design theme for publications. You can

focus on the content of the publication, because of its design

the decision has been made.

We have provided a template for the brochure that you will make.

Eat. From the template, you will create a new brochure,

add text, logos, and graphics.

The template has two pages. You will only work on the page

1 for creating a brochure in this tutorial. Once you finish, you can use the page

to create your own version of the brochure.

to open a brochure template:

Select Open from Menu: *File > New From Template.*

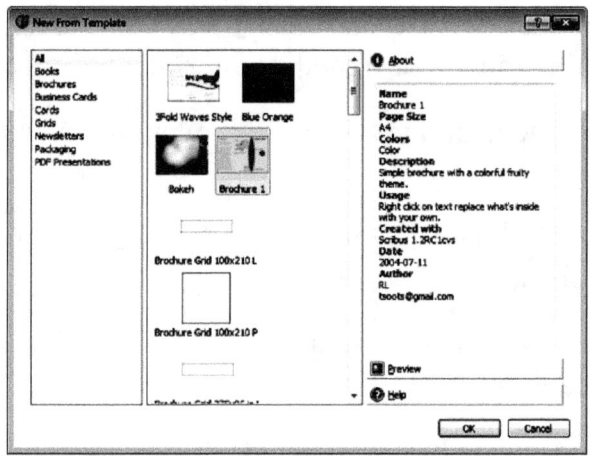

Click OK to open the file copy and get started.

An untitled publication window opens. Some of the work has been done for you: margins are set and some guides are positioned to create a design grid. Taking advantage of prebuilts is one of the advantages of using templates.

1. Create Columns

Everything you see on the page is actually on the page master. The master page contains design elements consisting of

mon to each page in the publication. Master pages provide the basis for most of the publications you create in SCRIBUS. They help build a consistent look within and between publications, and save you time.

You will modify this master page by adding guide columns, which you will use to position the text.

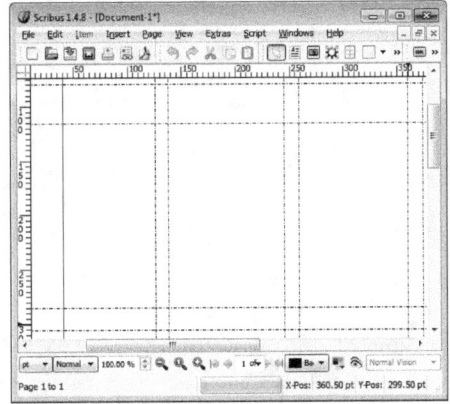

main page

Design elements on master pages appear on every page in the publication, but you can omit them from specific pages if necessary.

Column guides are non-printing vertical lines that allow

You align text and graphics in publications. Creating column guides on master pages ensures that columns are identical across publications. for this brochure, you will create four columns. to create a column:

Click the master page icon to move to the master page.

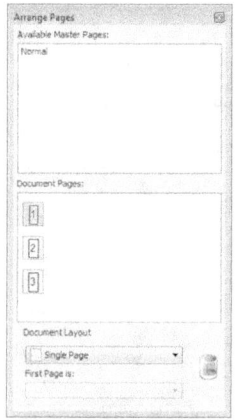

Select Column Wizard from

Menu: *Page > Manage Guide>Column Row.*

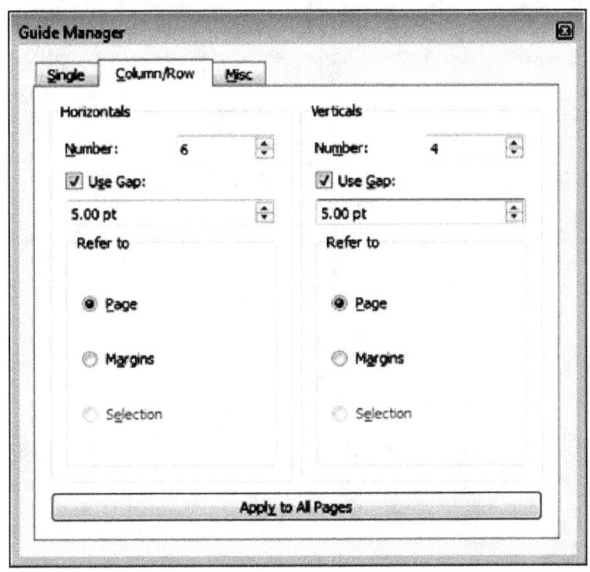

for Number of Columns, then press Tab or click in the text box Space Between Columns and Row.25 (.64cm)

4 Click OK to close the dialog box.

Column guides appear, dividing your page into four equal columns.

Brochure, after you create the columns.

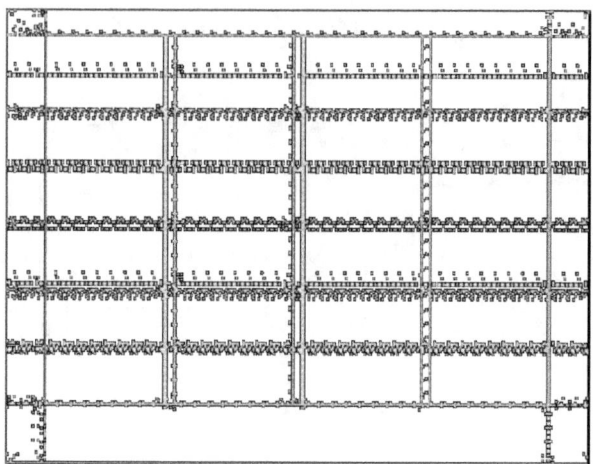

Click the page 1 icon to return to page 1, where you will do your work in this tutorial.

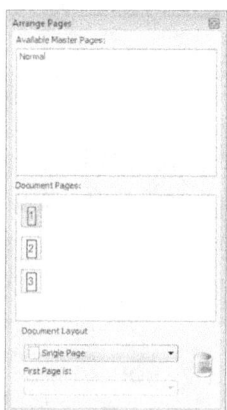

If you don't see column guides on page 1, select Copy Master Guides from the Layout menu (Layout > Copy Master Guides).

2. Importing Graphics

CRIBUS allows you to import graphics in a variety of formats, including SVG, EPS, JPG, PNG TIFF, and EPS (PostScript encapsulation).

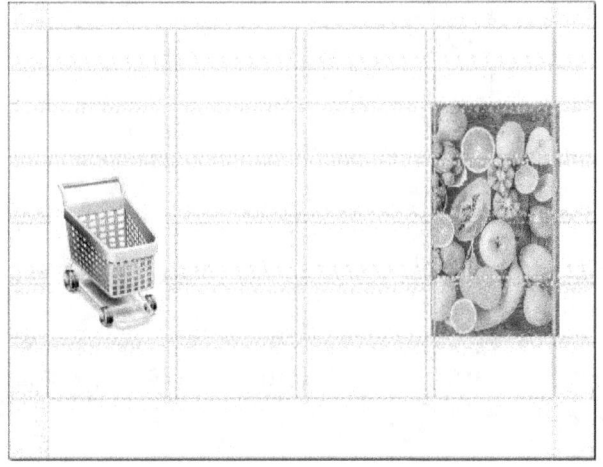

Brochure, after you place the image

The next step is to place one TIFF graphic on the right side of the page and a smaller

TIFF graphic on the left side of the page.

to place JPG graphics

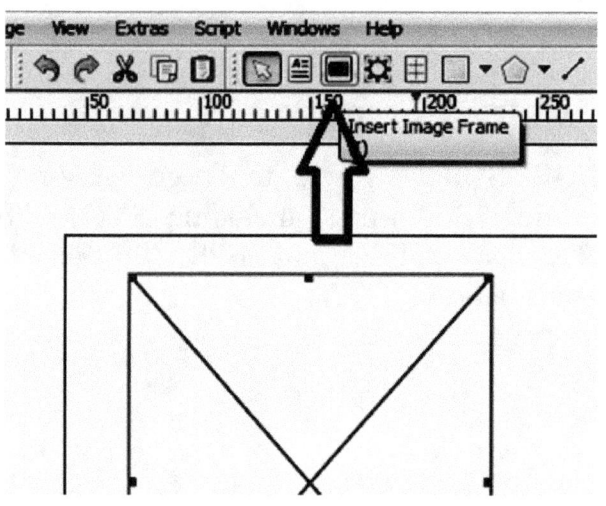

Gunakan Tool Insert Image frame pada toolbox.

Sengan cara, pilih Menu: *File > Import> Get Image (Ctrl + D)*

or right click Get Image.

file HAPPY SHOP.jpg then click OK

Position the loaded icon as shown below, then click at intersection 1-horizontal inches (4.5 cm) guide and the left edge of the third column to the chart place.

If the top left corner of the chart is not positioned as shown here, click the pointer on the graph and drag the graph into position. Top left corner of the graph should be positioned here

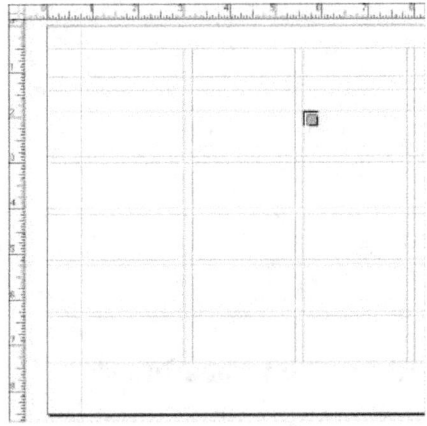

Pilih Menu: *File > Import> Get Image (Ctrl + D)*

or right click Get Image.

Select the Kopi.jpg file then click OK

Position the loaded icon as shown, then
click on intersection

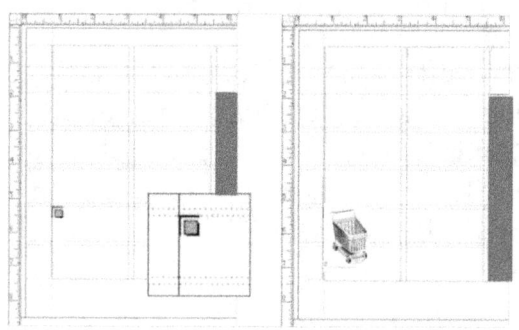

4

-inci (13,3 cm) horizontal

guide and left margin.

3. Creating and installing headings

Now you will create a block of text where
you will type towards the brochure.

You will position the title expand the first
three columns.

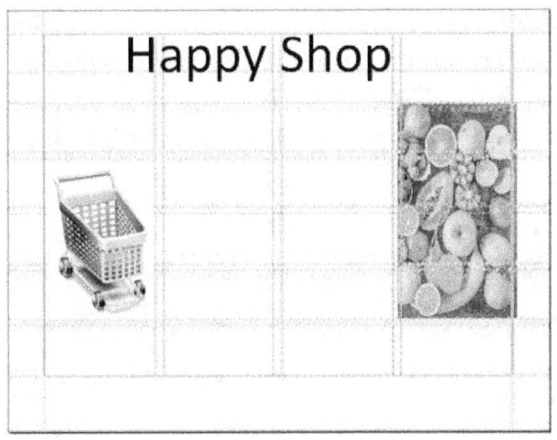

Brochure, after you add the title to type and position a heading:

Select the text tool and position the I-beam at the intersection of the top and left margin guides.

Drag the I-beam diagonally to define the text block.

Drag from the 1 inch (2.5 cm) mark on the ruler's horizontal line to the right edge of the third column and down to

1 inch marks (3.2 cm) on a vertical ruler.

When you release the mouse button, you will see the cursor flashes at your starting position.

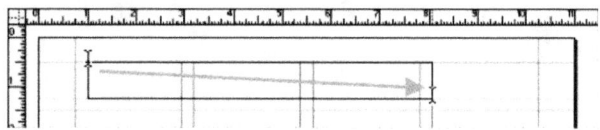

Type

"Happy Shop"

Notes:

You may want to change the view by selecting 75% The size of the Appearance submenu in the Layout menu.

If HAPPY SHOP is not already highlighted, select the text

tool and double-click the word HAPPY SHOP to select it.

Chose *Property>Text>Justify*

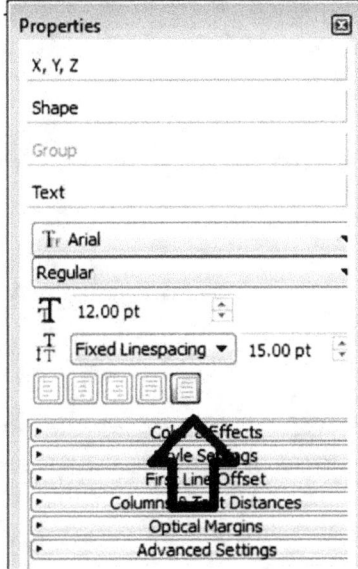

This distributes the characters evenly over the width block text.

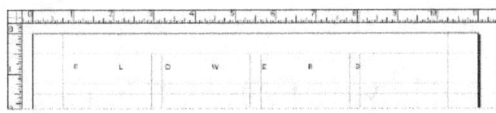

Select Character Style from

Menu: *Edit > Style >Character Style,*

and set the type attribute to match the existing one

The Type Specification dialog box is displayed here.

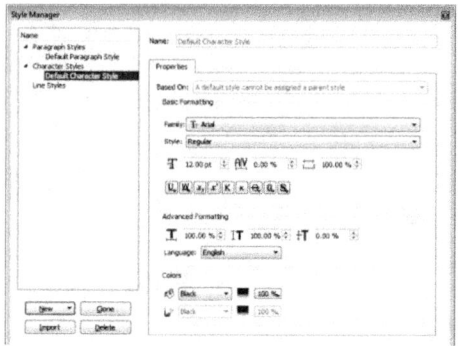

If Helvetica (from MAC) is not available, choose Arial (Windows) or another font.

Click Done to close the dialog box.

You may need to adjust the position of the title or the width of the text block to fit the illustration below. Use the pointer tool to select a block of text and position left/.

 inch (0.6 cm) between the letter H and the left page margins, and position the base line of the letters (imaginary line where the letters lie) on the horizontal guide at 1-inch (3.2 cm) marks on the vertical ruler.

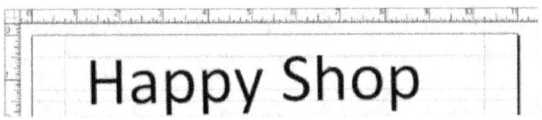

4. Change the Type Style and AlignmentYou can use commands on the Type menu to format text. Some of these commands (Font, Size, and Style Type, for example) apply to characters. Other commands (such as Paragraph, Indents/Tabs, and Alignment), apply to the entire paragraph. To make changes to a particular character or paragraph, the text tool must be selected and the character must be highlighted, or inserted

point must be clicked within the paragraph. If you select more than one paragraph, the changes will apply to all selected paragraphs.

Note:

If you select the command from the Type with-any selected character or paragraph menu, you will reset the default attributes, which will apply to all new text you type.

Some formatting commands apply to paragraphs (for example, graphic paraspacing, indentation, tabbing, and alignment). Here we use the Align ment command to center the paragraph.

5. Using the Control Palette

The Control Palette is an alternative to moving, resizing, and rotating elements manually. Using the Control palette, you have precise control over text and graphics and can make multiple changes without changing tools or selecting commands.

The settings and options available in the Control palette change according to what you select in the SCRIBUS window.

When you select graphics and text blocks with the pointing tool, you can enter precise numerical values ??in the Controls palette to move, resize, rotate, scale, and crop the objects. When you click in a text block with a text tool, you can apply formatting to text and paragraphs.

In this tutorial, you will use the Control palette to precisely rotate blocks of text in a brochure.

Property Control:

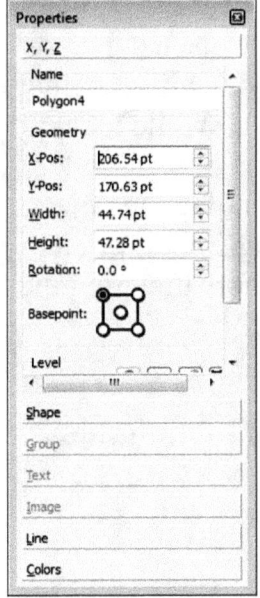

Control properties of selected objects. Control Properties of selected text.

6. Rotate And Move Text Blocks

SCRIBUS provides extensive control over objects in your publications. You can precisely position graphics and text blocks, rotate them in 0.01 degree increments, and resize them to your exact specifications.

You can rotate an object (text or graphic) by using the rotate tool in the toolbox, the Rotate option in the Controls palette, or both. for this exercise, you will use the rotate tool to rotate an object, while looking at the rotation angle in the Control palette. When you have finished binding the object, you will set the rotation angle appropriately with the Control palette before dragging the object into position in the flyer.

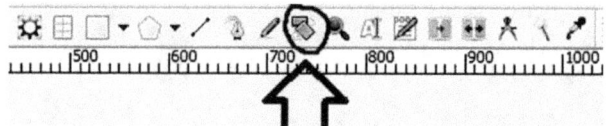

First, create a Text Text block and Click the Spinner Icon in the Toolbox.:

Select the text tool, move to the whiteboard

(as shown), then drag to create a block of text about 1 inch (2.5cm) wide and (1.3cm) long.

Type 'SALE"

With the text selected, format it in 14-point Helvetica using the Size command on the Type *menu (Type > Size).*

Now you will rotate and move the text block:

Use the zoom tool to enlarge the area around the word SALE and the letter H in HAPPY SHOP,

1.861 / 5.000

To rotate an object, click on the toolbox with the image below.

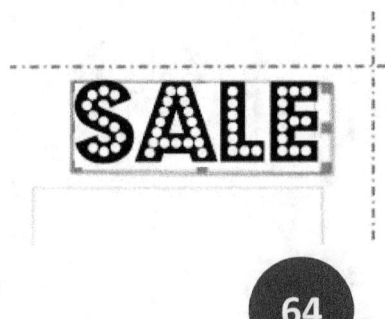

Text blocks have windows
handles at the top and bottom,
indicates that it is selected.

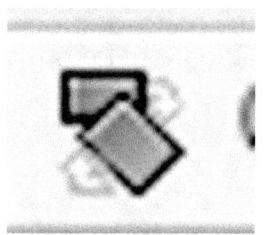

Select the rotate tool, and position it
starburst in the middle of a text block.
The location in the text block where you
clicked starburst is called a fixed point.
Rotate objects, moving it around its fixed
point.

Keep turning until the baseline is SALE
aligned with the left edge of HAPPY SHOP
and the rotation angle indicated on the
Control palette is appropriate
approximately 90 degrees.

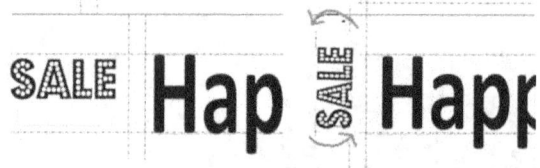

You may need to move SALE closer to HAPPY SHOP view and align both blocks of text. Select the pointer tool and drag the SALE text block closer to HAPPY SHOP.

To ensure that the rotation angle is exactly 90 degrees, make sure the number displayed in the Rotate option on the Control palette is 90. If not, type 90, and then press Enter .

Next, rotate the option with the Proprrty Geometry Tool for a more precise 90 degrees.

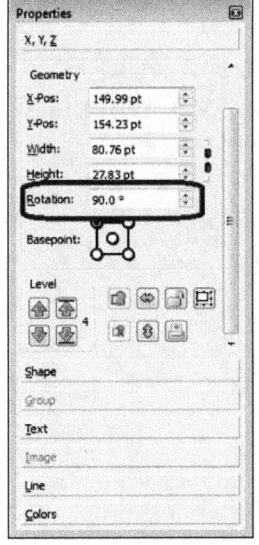

Select the pointing tool, and click the SALE text block again.

Drag the rotated text block to the position next to the H in HAPPY SHOP, as shown below. The bottom of the letter in SALE should rest on the Happy bottom line.

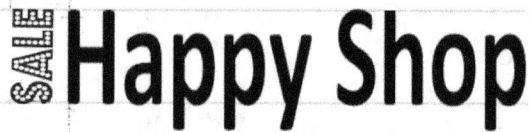

7. Placing Text Files

Placing text in SCRIBUS is similar to placing graphics. in this step, you will place the text file in the brochure.

view the entire brochure, select Fit in Window from

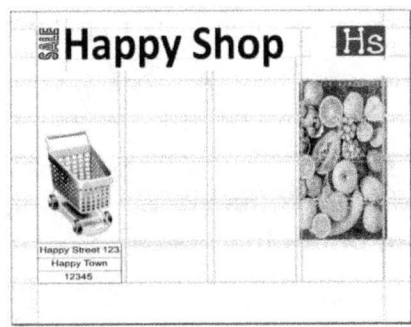

View submenu on the Layout menu.
(*Layout >View > Fits on Window*)

Brochure, after you place the first column of the text file to place the first column of text: Make sure there is no check mark next to it

Autoflow command.. If present, select Autoflow to deselect.

Autoflow is useful for flowing all the text in a file into a publication file. However, in this case, you want to place the text column by column.

Position the loaded text icon at the intersection of the left margin and the horizontal guide at a distance of 2 inches (5 cm) marked on the ruler, then click to place the text.

The down arrow at the bottom of the window handle indicates there is more text to place.

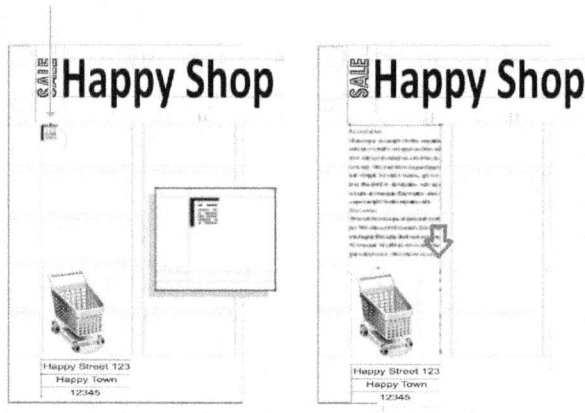

Loaded text icon

When you click the loaded text icon, the text flows from the point where you clicked to the bottom of the column.

8. Create Multiple Text Blocks

Interrelated

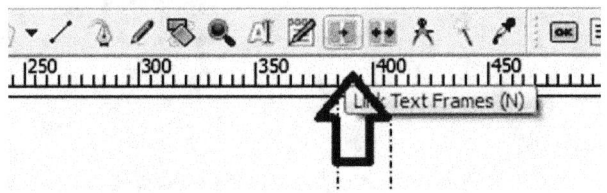

One of the strongest features in SCRIBUS is:

-flexibility.

-text block capability.

You can flow text from one writing block to another, splitting it up, and changing its shape as a page layout and graphic image in the publication you are writing, while continuing to create a complete manuscript flow.

Brochure, after you place the second text block In SCRIBUS, you can create separate blocks of text in the same story to accommodate any page design. This

Threaded blocks of text can be on the same or different pages

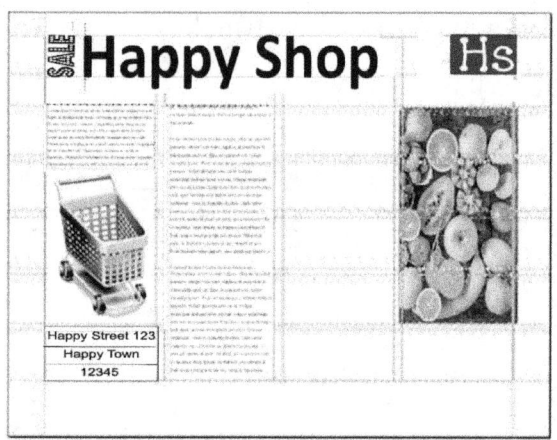

ent page. In this exercise, you will flow a second block of text from the same story into the second column of the brochure.

to flow text into the second column:

Using the pointing tool, drag the bottom window1

from the text block to the -inch mark (13cm) on the vertical ruler.

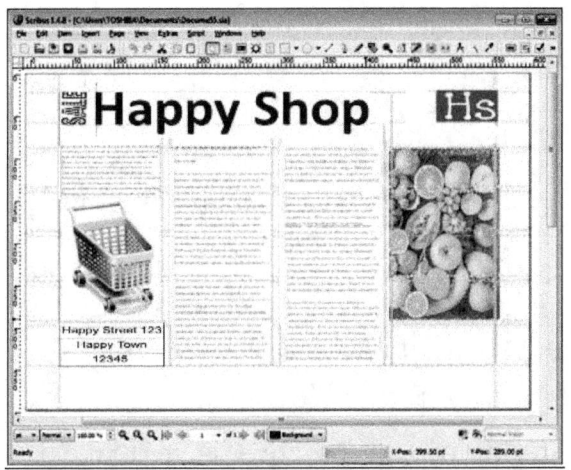

When you move the window curtain up, the text block is shorter. This is called

"roll up the window blinds."

Click the down arrow in the bottom window address. A loaded text icon appears.

Position the loaded text icon on the left edge second column on the 2 inch (5 cm) horizontal guide, and click to place the text.

The text flows into the second column.

Roll the bottom window of the second text

block until both text columns are the same length.

Dragging To Place Text

Now you will create the final block of text. The process you will carry out

Using drag placement allows you to place text anywhere in the area you specify, even across multiple columns.

The result of our practice is to make the Flyer ready.

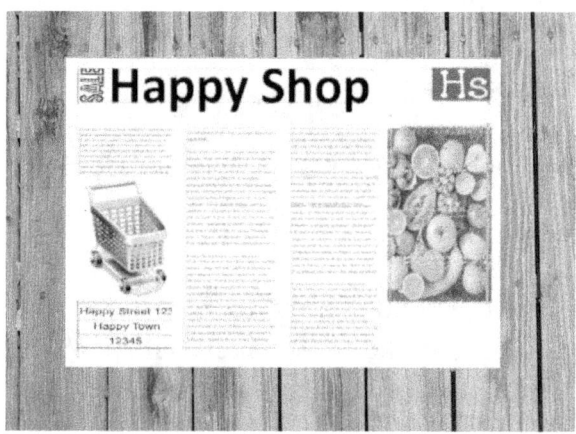

Thank You